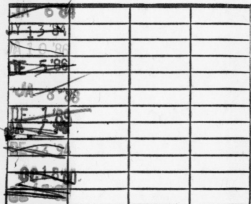

THE TREASURY OF CHRISTMAS MUSIC

THE TREASURY OF
CHRISTMAS MUSIC

Edited by

W. L. REED
Mus.Doc.

LONDON

BLANDFORD PRESS

Published 1950

Copyright © 1961 Blandford Press Ltd,
167 High Holborn, London WC1V 6PH

Second Impression 1951
Third Impression 1956
Fourth Impression 1961
Fifth Impression 1966
Sixth Impression 1973
(58th thousand)

ISBN 0 7137 0263 X

ACKNOWLEDGEMENT

Acknowledgement is due to the various owners
of copyright whose material is reproduced in this
volume by kind permission.

Detailed acknowledgement is given at the foot of
the pieces where applicable.

Printed in Great Britain by
Lowe & Brydone (Printers) Ltd., Thetford, Norfolk

Contents

Foreword

I have recollections of carol singing occasions when delightful programmes have been produced, but where the singers have been in difficulties to keep track of all the many small pieces of paper which they were using for their work. Dr. Reed has, in this book, endeavoured to collect all the carols that might be wanted for occasions of this kind and put them conveniently together. I think that users will find here practically every carol that they are normally likely to need. The word traditional, as applied to the first section in the book, has a wide application.

I hope this collection may be of use and value to very many carol singers, and also be the means of introducing hitherto unknown tunes to those who will assuredly come to love them.

ADRIAN C. BOULT

1. A CHILD THIS DAY IS BORN

Traditional   Traditional, arr. W. L. R.

mf
1. A Child this day is born,—— A Child of high re - nown, Most
2. These ti - dings shep - herds heard,—— In field watch-ing their fold, Most

wor - thy of a scep - tre, A scep - tre and a crown:
by an an - gel un - to them That night re - vealed and told:

CHORUS

f Now - ell, Now - ell, Now - ell, Now - ell, sing all we may, Be -

cause the King of all—— kings Was born this bless - èd day.

3. To whom the angel spoke,
   Saying, "Be not afraid;
   Be glad, poor silly shepherds—
   Why are you so dismayed?"

4. "For lo! I bring you tidings
   Of gladness and of mirth,
   Which cometh to all people by
   This holy Infant's birth."

5. Then was there with the angel
   An host incontinent
   Of heavenly bright soldiers,
   Which from the Highest was sent:

6. Lauding the Lord our God,
   And His celestial King;
   All glory be in Paradise,
   This heavenly host did sing:

7. And as the angel told them,
   So to them did appear;
   They found the young Child, Jesus Christ,
   With Mary, His Mother dear:

2. A LITTLE CHILD ON THE EARTH HAS BEEN BORN

Old Flemish, trans. R.C. Trevelyan*   Old Flemish, arr. W. L.R.

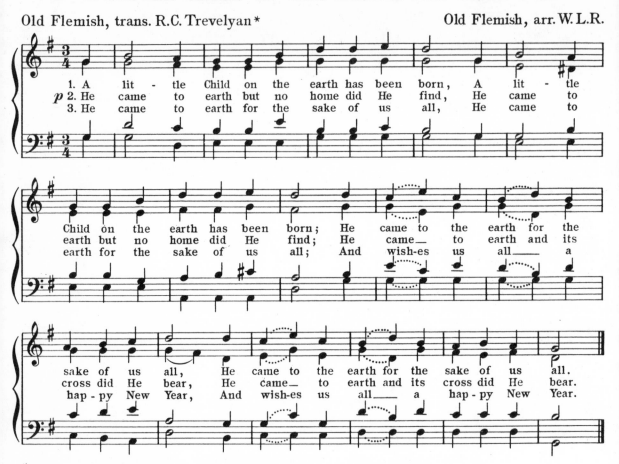

1. A lit-tle Child on the earth has been born, A lit-tle
2. He came to earth but no home did He find, He came to
3. He came to earth for the sake of us all, He came to

Child on the earth has been born; He came to the earth for the
earth but no home did He find; He came to earth and its
earth for the sake of us all; And wish-es us all a

sake of us all, He came to the earth for the sake of us all.
cross did He bear, He came to earth and its cross did He bear.
hap-py New Year, And wish-es us all a hap-py New Year.

From the Oxford Book of Carols, by permission of The Oxford University Press

3. ANGELS, FROM THE REALMS OF GLORY

James Montgomery (1771-1854) *with chorus altered*   French melody, arr. W. L.R.

1. An-gels, from the realms of glo-ry, Wing your flight o'er all the earth; Ye, who sang cre-
2. Shepherds in the field a-bid-ing, Watching o'er your flocks by night, God with man is

CHORUS

a-tion's sto-ry, Now proclaim Mes-si-ah's birth: f Glo -
now re-sid-ing; Yonder shines the In-fant light:

3. Sages, leave your contemplations;
   Brighter visions beam afar;
   Seek the great Desire of Nations;
   Ye have seen His natal star:

4. Saints before the altar bending,
   Watching long in hope and fear,
   Suddenly the Lord, descending,
   In His temple shall appear:

4. AS WITH GLADNESS MEN OF OLD

William Chatterton Dix (1837-1898)

Conrad Kocher (1786-1872)

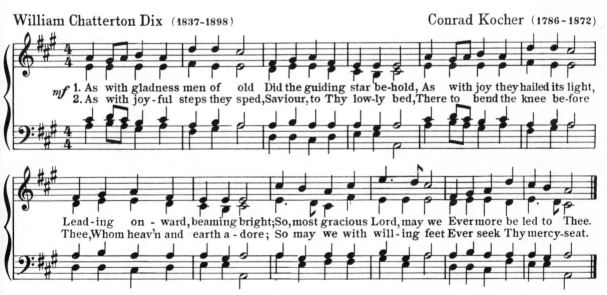

3. As they offered gifts most rare
   At Thy cradle rude and bare;
   So may we with holy joy,
   Pure, and free from sin's alloy,
   All our costliest treasures bring,
   Christ, to Thee, our heavenly King.

4. Holy Jesus, every day
   Keep us in the narrow way;
   And, when earthly things are past,
   Bring our ransomed souls at last
   Where they need no star to guide,
   Where no clouds Thy glory hide.

5. In the heavenly country bright
   Need they no created light;
   Thou its Light, its Joy, its Crown,
   Thou its Sun which goes not down;
   There for ever may we sing
   Hallelujahs to our King.

5. A VIRGIN MOST PURE

Traditional   Traditional

1. A Vir-gin most pure, as the pro-phets do tell, Hath brought forth a
2. At Beth-lem in Jew-ry a — ci-ty there was Where Jos-eph and

Ba-by, as it hath be-fel, To be our Re-deem-er from death, hell and
Ma-ry to-geth-er did pass, All for to be tax-èd with ma-ny one

CHORUS

sin, Which A-dam's trans-gress-ion hath wrap-pèd us in. ƒ And there-fore be
moe, For Cae-sar com-mand-ed the same should be so.

mer-ry, set sor-row a-side; Christ Jes-us our Sav-iour was born on this tide.

3. But when they had entered the city so fair,
A number of people so mighty was there,
That Joseph and Mary, whose substance was small,
Could find in the inn there no lodging at all.

4. Then were they constrainèd in a stable to lie,
Where horses and asses they used for to tie;
Their lodging so simple they took it no scorn,
But against the next morning our Saviour was born.

5. The King of all kings to this world being brought,
Small store of fine linen to wrap Him was sought,
But when She had swaddled Her young Son so sweet,
Within an ox-manger She laid Him to sleep.

6. Then God sent an angel from heaven so high
To certain poor shepherds in fields where they lie,
And bade them no longer in sorrow to stay,
Because that our Saviour was born on this day.

7. Then presently after the shepherds did spy
A number of angels that stood in the sky;
They joyfully talkèd and sweetly did sing,
To God be all glory, our heavenly King.

6. AWAY IN A MANGER

Anon.

W. J. Kirkpatrick (1838-1921)

Slowly

S.
A.
(or unison)

1. A - way in a man - ger, no crib for a bed, The
2. The cat - tle are low - ing, the Ba - by a - wakes, But
3. Be near me, Lord Jes - us; I ask Thee to stay Close

lit - tle Lord Jes - us laid down His sweet head. The
lit - tle Lord Jes - us no cry - ing He makes. I
by me for ev - er, and love me, I pray. Bless

stars in the bright sky looked down where He lay, The
love Thee, Lord Jes - us! Look down from the sky And
all the dear chil - dren in Thy ten - der care, And

lit - tle Lord Jes - us a - sleep on the hay.
stay by my side un - til morn - ing is nigh.
fit us for hea - ven, to live with Thee there.

7. BESIDE THY CRADLE HERE I STAND

Chorale from
J.S.Bach's 'Christmas Oratorio'

8. BREAK FORTH, O BEAUTEOUS, HEAVENLY LIGHT

Chorale from
J. S. Bach's 'Christmas Oratorio'

9. BRIGHTEST AND BEST OF THE SONS OF THE MORNING

Reginald Heber (1783-1826)

J. F. Thrupp (1827-1867)

1. Bright-est and best of the sons of the morn-ing,
2. Cold on His cra-dle the dew-drops are shin-ing;

Dawn on our dark-ness, and lend us thine aid;
Low lies His head with the beasts of the stall;

Star of the East,— the hor-i-zon a-dorn-ing,—
An-gels a-dore— Him in slum-ber re-clin-ing,—

Guide— where our In-fant Re-deem-er is laid.
Mak-er, and Mon-arch, and Sav-iour of all.

3. Say, shall we yield Him, in costly devotion,
Odours of Edom, and offerings divine,
Gems of the mountain, and pearls of the ocean,
Myrrh from the forest, or gold from the mine?

4. Vainly we offer each ample oblation;
Vainly with gifts would His favour secure;
Richer by far is the heart's adoration;
Dearer to God are the prayers of the poor.

Unis. 5. Brightest and best of the sons of the morning,
Dawn on our darkness, and lend us thine aid;
Star of the East, the horizon adorning,
Guide where our Infant Redeemer is laid.

10. CHRISTIANS, AWAKE, SALUTE THE HAPPY MORN

John Byrom (1691-1763)   J. Wainwright (1723-1768)

3. He spake; and straightway the celestial choir
In hymns of joy, unknown before, conspire.
The praises of redeeming love they sang,
And heav'n's whole orb with Alleluias rang;
God's highest glory was their anthem still,
Peace upon earth, and unto men goodwill.

4. O may we keep and ponder in our mind
God's wondrous love in saving lost mankind;
Trace we the Babe, Who hath retrieved our loss,
From the poor manger to the bitter Cross;
Tread in His steps, assisted by His grace,
Till man's first heav'nly state again takes place.

5. Then may we hope, the angelic hosts among,
To sing, redeemed, a glad triumphal song;
He that was born upon this joyful day
Around us all His glory shall display;
Saved by His love, incessant we shall sing
Eternal praise to heav'n's almighty King.

11. COME ALL YOU WORTHY GENTLEMEN

Traditional*

English Folk Carol, arr. H.A.C.

1. Come all you wor-thy gen-tle-men That may be standing by,— Christ our bless-èd
2. Christ our blessèd Sav - iour Now in the manger lay— He's ly - ing in the
3. God bless the rul-er of this house, And long on may he reign, Ma-ny hap-py

Sav - iour Was born on Christ-mas day. The bless-èd Vir - gin Ma - ry Un-
man-ger, While the ox - en feed on hay. The bless-èd Vir - gin Ma - ry Un-
Christ-mas - es He live to see a - gain! God bless our gen-er - a - tion Who

to the Lord did say, O we wish you the com - fort and tid - ings of joy!
to the Lord did say, O we wish you the com - fort and tid - ings of joy!
live both far and near, And we wish them a hap - py, a hap - py New Year!

* By permission of Novello & Co. Ltd.

12. DING DONG! MERRILY ON HIGH

From 'Orchésographie' (Thoinot Arbeau, 1588)
harm. Charles Wood

G. R. Woodward

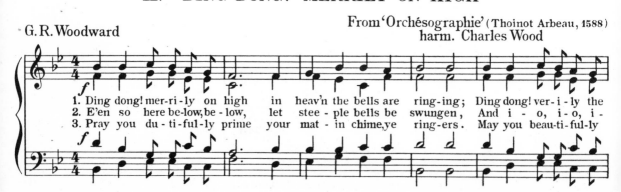

1. Ding dong! mer-ri-ly on high in heav'n the bells are ring-ing; Ding dong! ver-i-ly the
2. E'en so here be-low, be-low, let stee-ple bells be swungen, And i - o, i - o, i -
3. Pray you du-ti-ful-ly prime your mat - in chime, ye ring-ers. May you beau-ti-ful-ly

sky   is   riv'n with an - gel   sing - ing.
o,   by   priest and peo - ple   sung - en.   Glo - - - - - - -
rime   your   eve - time song, ye   sing - ers;

- ri - a, Ho - san - na in ex - cel - sis!

From the Cambridge Carol Book, by permission of the S.P.C.K.

13. DOWN IN YON FOREST

Traditional *   English Folk Carol, arr. W. L. R.

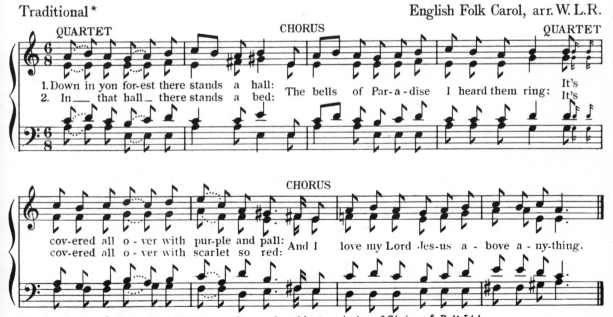

1. Down in yon for - est there stands a   hall: The bells of Par - a - dise I heard them ring: It's
2. In___ that hall___ there stands a   bed: It's

cov - ered all o - ver with pur - ple and pall: And I   love my Lord Jes - us a - bove a - ny - thing.
cov - ered all o - ver with scarlet so red:

By permission of R. Vaughan Williams and reproduced by permission of Stainer & Bell Ltd.

3. At the bed-side there lies a stone:
   The bells of Paradise I heard them ring:
   Which the sweet Virgin Mary knelt upon:
   And I love my Lord Jesus above anything.

4. Under that bed there runs a flood:
   The bells of Paradise I heard them ring:
   The one half runs water, the other runs blood:
   And I love my Lord Jesus above anything.

5. At the bed's foot there grows a thorn:
   The bells of Paradise I heard them ring:
   Which ever blows blossom since He was born:
   And I love my Lord Jesus above anything.

6. Over that bed the moon shines bright:
   The bells of Paradise I heard them ring:
   Denoting our Saviour was born this night:
   And I love my Lord Jesus above anything.

14. GOD BLESS THE MASTER OF THIS HOUSE
(FURRY DAY CAROL)

Traditional

Traditional Cornish, arr. H.A.C.

With spirit

1. God bless the mas-ter of this house, And all that are there-in-a, And
2. Then let us all most mer-ry be, And sing with cheer-ful voice-a, For
3. Then sing with voic-es cheerful-ly, For Christ this time was born-a, Who

to be-gin this Christ-mas-tide With mirth now let us sing-a!
we have good oc-ca-sion now This time for to re-joice-a. The
did from death de-liv-er us When we were left for-lorn-a. The

Sav-iour of all peo-ple Up-on this time was born-a, Who

did from death de-liv-er us, When we were left for-lorn-a.

15. GOD REST YOU MERRY, GENTLEMEN

Traditional

Traditional

mf 1. God rest you mer-ry, gen-tle-men, Let no-thing you dis-may, Re-mem-ber Christ our
2. In Beth-le-hem in Jew-ry This bless-èd Babe was born, And laid with-in a

Sav - iour Was born on Christ-mas day; To save us all from Sa-tan's pow'r When
man - ger Up - on this bless-èd morn; The which His Mo-ther Ma - ry Did

CHORUS

we were gone a stray: _ff_ O___ ti - dings of com - fort and
no - thing take in scorn:

joy, comfort and joy, O___ ti - dings of com - fort and joy.

3. From God our heavenly Father
     A blessèd angel came,
   And unto certain shepherds
     Brought tidings of the same,
   How that in Bethlehem was born
     The Son of God by name:

4. ' Fear not,' then said the angel,
     ' Let nothing you affright,
   This day is born a Saviour
     Of a pure Virgin bright,
   To free all those who trust in Him
     From Satan's power and might,'

5. The shepherds at those tidings
     Rejoicèd much in mind,
   And left their flocks a-feeding
     In tempest, storm and wind,
   And went to Bethlehem straightway
     This blessèd Babe to find:

6. But when to Bethlehem they came,
     Whereat this Infant lay,
   They found Him in a manger,
     Where oxen feed on hay;
   His Mother Mary kneeling,
     Unto the Lord did pray:

7. Now to the Lord sing praises,
     All you within this place,
   And with true love and brotherhood
     Each other now embrace;
   This holy tide of Christmas
     All others doth deface;

16. GOOD CHRISTIAN MEN, REJOICE

Latin, *(In dulci jubilo)*
trans. John Mason Neale (1818-1866)

German, 14th Century

1. Good Christ-ian men, re - joice ___ With heart and soul and voice! ___
2. Good Christ-ian men, re - joice ___ With heart and soul and voice! ___
3. Good Christ-ian men, re - joice ___ With heart and soul and voice! ___

Give ye heed to what we say: News! News! Je - sus Christ is
Now ye hear of end - less bliss: Joy! Joy! Je - sus Christ was
Now ye need not fear the grave: Peace! Peace! Je - sus Christ was

born to - day. Ox and ass be - fore Him bow, And He is in the
born for this. He hath oped the heav'n-ly door, And man is blessed for
born to save, Calls you one, and calls you all, To gain His ev - er -

man - ger now. Christ is born to - day! ___ Christ is born to - day! ___
ev - er-more. Christ was born for this! ___ Christ was born for this! ___
last-ing hall. Christ was born to save! ___ Christ was born to save! ___

17. GOOD KING WENCESLAS

John Mason Neale (1818-1866)

Piae Cantiones (1582)
arr. W. L. R.

1. Good King Wen - ces - las looked out, On the Feast of Steph - en,
2. 'Hith - er, page, and stand by me, If thou know'st it, tell - ing,

When the snow lay round a - bout, Deep and crisp and e - ven;
Yon - der pea - sant, who is he? Where and what his dwell - ing?'

Bright - ly shone the moon that night, Though the frost was cru - el,
'Sire, he lives a good league hence, Un - der - neath the moun - tain,

When a poor man came in sight, Gath'ring win - ter fu - el.
Right a - gainst the for - est fence, By Saint Ag - nes' foun - tain.'

3. 'Bring me flesh, and bring me wine,
    Bring me pine logs hither:
Thou and I will see him dine,
    When we bear them thither.'
Page and monarch, forth they went,
    Forth they went together
Through the rude wind's wild lament
    And the bitter weather.

4. 'Sire, the night is darker now,
    And the wind blows stronger;
Fails my heart, I know not how;
    I can go no longer.'
'Mark my footsteps, good my page,
    Tread thou in them boldly;
Thou shalt find the winter's rage
    Freeze thy blood less coldly.'

5. In his master's steps he trod,
    Where the snow lay dinted;
Heat was in the very sod
    Which the Saint had printed.
Therefore, Christian men, be sure,
    Wealth or rank possessing,
Ye who now will bless the poor,
    Shall yourselves find blessing.

B.P. 103

18. HARK! THE HERALD ANGELS SING

Charles Wesley (1707-1788)

F. Mendelssohn (1809-1847)

1. Hark! the her - ald an-gels sing — Glo - ry to the new-born King,
2. Christ, by high - est heav'n a - dored, Christ, the ev - er - last - ing Lord,
3. Hail the heav'n - born Prince of Peace! Hail the Sun of Right-eous - ness!

Peace on earth, and mer - cy mild, — God and sin - ners re - con - ciled.
Late in time be - hold Him come, — Off-spring of a Vir - gin's womb!
Light and life to all He brings, Ris'n with heal - ing in His wings.

Joy - ful, all ye na - tions, rise, — Join the tri - umph of the skies; —
Veiled in flesh the God-head see; — Hail th'in - car - nate De - i - ty! —
Mild He lays His glo - ry by, — Born that man no more may die, —

With th'an - gel - ic host pro-claim, Christ is born in Beth - le - hem.
Pleased as Man with men to dwell, Je - sus, our Im - man - u - el.
Born to raise the sons of earth, Born to give them se - cond birth.

Hark! the her - ald an - gels sing — Glo - ry to the new-born King.

Organ

19.   HE SMILES WITHIN HIS CRADLE

Austrian, trans. Robert Graves *

Austrian, arr. W.L.R.

1. He smiles with-in His cra - dle, A Babe with face so bright _____ It beams most like a mir - ror A - gainst a blaze of light: _____ This Babe so burn - ing bright. _____

2. This Babe we now de-clare to you Is Je - sus Christ our Lord; _____ He brings both peace and heart - i - ness. Haste, haste with one ac - cord _____ To feast with Christ our Lord. _____

From the Oxford Book of Carols, by permission of The Oxford University Press

3. And who would rock the cradle
   Wherein this Infant lies,
   Must rock with easy motion
   And watch with humble eyes,
   Like Mary pure and wise.

4. O Jesus, dearest Babe of all
   And dearest Babe of mine,
   Thy love is great, Thy limbs are small.
   O, flood this heart of mine
   With overflow from Thine!

20. I KNOW A ROSE TREE SPRINGING

(Es ist ein' Ros' entsprungen)

Speier Gebetbuch (1599)

German Traditional Melody

Gently, but with movement

1. I know a rose-tree spring-ing Forth from an an-cient root, As men of old were sing-ing. From Jes-se came the shoot That bore a blos-som bright ___ A-mid the cold of win-ter, When half-spent was the night.

2. This rose-tree, blos-som-la-den, Where-of I-sa-iah spake, Is Ma-ry, spot-less Maid-en, Who mo-thered, for our sake, The lit-tle Child, new-born ___ By God's e-ter-nal coun-sel On that first Christ-mas morn.

3. O Flow'r, Whose fra-grance ten-der With sweet-ness fills the air, Dis-pel in glo-rious splen-dour The dark-ness ev-'ry-where; True man, yet ve-ry God, ___ From sin and death now save us, And share our ev-'ry load.

By permission of the Church Pension Fund, 20 Exchange Place, New York 5, N.Y., U.S.A.

1. *Es ist ein' Ros' entsprungen*
   Aus einer Wurzel zart,
   Als uns die Alten sungen:
   Aus Jesse kam die Art;
   Und hat ein Blümlein bracht,
   Mitten im kalten Winter,
   Wohl zu der halben Nacht.

2. *Das Röslein, das ich meine,*
   Davon Jesaias sagt,
   Ist Maria die reine,
   Die uns dies Blümlein bracht;
   Aus Gottes ew'gem Rat
   Hat sie ein Kindlein g'boren,
   Ist blieb'n ein' reine Magd.

3. *Wir bitten dich von Herzen,*
   Maria, Rose zart,
   Durch dieses Blümlein's Schmerzen,
   Die er empfunden hat,
   Wollst uns behülflich sein,
   Dass wir ihm mögen machen
   Ein' Wohnung hübsch und fein!

21. I SAW THREE SHIPS

Traditional

Allegretto

Traditional, arr. H.A.C.

Verses 1,3,5,7,9.

1. I saw three ships come sail-ing in, On Christ-mas Day, on Christ-mas Day; I

last Verse rall.

saw three ships come sail-ing in, On Christ - mas Day in the morn - ing.

Verses 2,4,6,8.

On Christ-mas Day, on Christ-mas Day?

2. And what was in those ships all three, On Christ - mas Day? And

On Christ - mas Day in the morn - ing?

what was in those ships all three,

3. Our Saviour Christ and His Lady,
   On Christmas Day, on Christmas Day;
   Our Saviour Christ and His Lady,
   On Christmas Day in the morning.

4. Pray, whither sailed those ships all three?

5. O, they sailed into Bethlehem.

6. And all the bells on earth shall ring.

7. And all the angels in Heaven shall sing.

8. And all the souls on earth shall sing.

9. Then let us all rejoice amain!

22. IN DULCI JUBILO

German, trans. R.L.Pearsall

R.L.Pearsall
arr. W.J.Westbrook

Soprano

1. In dul-ci ju-bi-lo ___ Let us our hom-age shew; ___
2. O Je-su par-vu-le! ___ My heart is sore for Thee! ___

Alto

1. In dul-ci ju-bi-lo ___ Let us our hom-age shew; ___
2. O Je-su par-vu-le! ___ My heart is sore for Thee! ___

Tenor

1. In dul-ci ju-bi-lo ___ Let us our hom-age shew; ___
2. O Je-su par-vu-le! ___ My heart is sore for Thee! ___

Bass

1. In dul-ci ju-bi-lo ___ Let us our hom-age shew; ___
2. O Je-su par-vu-le! ___ My heart is sore for Thee! ___

Piano *(for rehearsal only)*

Our heart's joy re-cli - neth In præ-se - pi - o, ___ And like a bright star
Hear me, I be-seech ___ Thee, O Puer op - ti - me! ___ My pray-er let it

Our heart's joy re-cli - neth In præ-se - pi - o, ___ And like a bright star
Hear me, I be-seech ___ Thee, O Puer op - ti - me! ___ My pray-er let it

Our heart's joy re-cli - neth In præ-se - pi - o, ___ And like a bright star
Hear me, I be-seech ___ Thee, O Puer op - ti - me! ___ My pray-er let it

Our heart's joy re-cli - neth In præ-se - pi - o, ___ And like a bright star
Hear me, I be-seech ___ Thee, O Puer op - ti - me! ___ My pray-er let it

34

Na - ti le - ni - tas! _____ Deep were _____ we stain-èd *Per no - stra*

Na - ti le - ni - tas! Deep - ly were _____ we stain - èd *Per no - stra*

- tas! _____ Deep - ly were we stain - èd *Per no - stra cri - mi - na;* _____

cri - mi - na; _____ But Thou hast for us gain-èd *Cœ - lo - rum gau - di -*

cri - mi - na; But Thou, _____ Thou hast gain - èd *Cœ - lo - rum gau - di -*

_____ But Thou hast for us gain - èd *Cœ - lo - rum gau - di - a:* _____

B.P. 103

*Small notes optional

23. IN THAT POOR STABLE
(Dans cette étable)
(Bethlehem)

Fléchier
trans. Maurice F. Bell*

French
arr. Charles Gounod

1. In that poor stable How charm-ing Je - sus lies, Words are not a - ble To fath-om His em-prise! No pal-ace of a king Can show so rare a thing__ In his-tor-y or fa-ble As that of which we sing In that poor sta - ble.

1. Dans cette é - ta - ble Que Jé - sus est char-mant, Qu'il est ai - ma - ble Dans cet a-bais-se-ment! Que d'at-traits à la fois! Tous les pa-lais des rois__ N'ont rien de com-pa-ra-ble Aux char-mes que je vois Dans cette é - ta - ble.

*From the Oxford Book of Carols, by permission of The Oxford University Press

2. See here God's power
In weakness fortifies
 This infant hour
Of Love's epiphanies!
Our foe is now despoiled,
The wiles of hell are foiled;
On earth there grows a flower
Pure, undefiled, unsoiled—
See here God's power!

3. Though far from knowing
The Babe's divinity,
 Mine eyes are growing
To see His majesty;
For lo! the new-born Child
Upon me sweetly smiled,
The gift of faith bestowing;
Thus I my Lord descry,
 Though far from knowing.

4. No more affliction!
For God endures our pains;
 In crucifixion
The Son victorious reigns.
For us the Sufferer brings
Salvation in His wings;
To win our souls' affection
Could He, the King of kings,
Know more affliction?

2. Que sa puissance
Paraît bien en ce jour,
 Malgré l'enfance
Où l'a réduit l'amour!
Notre ennemi dompté,
L'enfer déconcerté,
Font voir qu'en sa naissance
Rien n'est si redouté
Que sa puissance.

3. Sans le connaître,
Dans sa divinité
 Je vois paraître
Toute sa majesté;
Dans cet enfant qui naît,
À son aspect qui plaît,
Je découvre mon maître
Et je sens ce qu'il est
Sans le connaître.

4. Plus de misère!
Un Dieu souffre pour nous
 Et de son père
Appaise le courroux;
C'est en notre faveur
Qu'il naît dans la douleur;
Pouvait-il pour nous plaire
Unir à sa grandeur
Plus de misère?

24. IT CAME UPON THE MIDNIGHT CLEAR
(First Tune)

Edmund Hamilton Sears (1810–1876)

arr. Arthur Sullivan (1842–1900)

mf

1. It came up-on the midnight clear, That glo-rious song of old, From an-gels bend-ing near the earth To touch their harps of gold: "Peace on the earth, good-will to men, From heav'n's all-gracious King!" The world in sol-emn still-ness lay To hear the an-gels sing.

2. Still through the clo-ven skies they come With peaceful wings un-furled, And still their heav'nly mu-sic floats O'er all the wea-ry world; A-bove its sad and low-ly plains They bend on hov'ring wing, And ev-er o'er its Ba-bel sounds The blessèd an-gels sing.

By permission of Novello & Co. Ltd.

3. Yet with the woes of sin and strife
   The world has suffered long;
   Beneath the angel-strain have rolled
   Two thousand years of wrong;
   And man, at war with man, hears not
   The love-song which they bring.
   O hush the noise, ye men of strife,
   And hear the angels sing.

4. And ye, beneath life's crushing load,
   Whose forms are bending low,
   Who toil along the climbing way
   With weary steps and slow—
   Look up! for glad and golden hours
   Come swiftly on the wing;
   O rest beside the weary road,
   And hear the angels sing.

5. For lo! the days are hastening on,
   By prophet bards foretold,
   When with the ever-circling years
   Comes round the Age of Gold,
   When peace shall over all the earth
   Its ancient splendours fling,
   And the whole world give back the song
   Which now the angels sing.

25. IT CAME UPON THE MIDNIGHT CLEAR

(Second Tune)

Edmund Hamilton Sears (1810-1876)

Richard Storrs Willis

1. It came up-on the midnight clear, That glorious song of old, ___ From an-gels bend-ing near the earth To touch their harps of gold: ___ "Peace on the earth, good-will to men, From heav'n's all gracious King!" The world in sol-emn stillness lay To hear the an-gels sing.

2. Still through the clo-ven skies they come With peaceful wings un-furled, ___ And still their heav'nly mu-sic floats O'er all the wea-ry world; ___ A-bove its sad and low-ly plains They bend on hov'ring wing, ___ And ev-er o'er its Ba-bel sounds The blessèd an-gels sing.

By permission of The Church Pension Fund, 20. Exchange Place, New York 5, N.Y., U.S.A.

3. Yet with the woes of sin and strife
   The world has suffered long;
Beneath the angel-strain have rolled
   Two thousand years of wrong;
And man, at war with man, hears not
   The love-song which they bring.
O hush the noise, ye men of strife,
   And hear the angels sing.

4. And ye, beneath life's crushing load,
   Whose forms are bending low,
Who toil along the climbing way
   With weary steps and slow —
Look up! for glad and golden hours
   Come swiftly on the wing;
O rest beside the weary road,
   And hear the angels sing.

5. For lo! the days are hastening on,
   By prophet bards foretold,
When with the ever-circling years
   Comes round the Age of Gold,
When peace shall over all the earth
   Its ancient splendours fling,
And the whole world give back the song
   Which now the angels sing.

26. JOSEPH DEAREST, JOSEPH MINE

(SONG OF THE CRIB)

German, trans. N.S.T.
Moderately fast

German
arr. R. Vaughan Williams

VOICES in UNISON

1. (Mary) Jo-seph dear-est, Jo-seph mine, Help me cra-dle the Child di-vine;
2. (Joseph) Glad-ly, dear One, La-dy mine, Help I cra-dle this Child of Thine;

God re-ward thee and all that's thine In Par-a-dise, So prays the Moth-er Ma-ry.
God's own light on us both shall shine In Par-a-dise, As prays the Moth-er Ma-ry.

CHORUS

He came a-mong us at Christ-mas-tide, At Christ-mas-tide, In

Beth-le-hem; Men shall bring Him from far and wide Love's di-a-dem:

Je - sus, Je - sus, Lo, He comes, and loves, and saves, and frees us!

From the Oxford Book of Carols, by permission of The Oxford University Press

3. *Servant (1)*
   Peace to all that have goodwill!
   God, Who heaven and earth doth fill,
   Comes to turn us away from ill,
   And lies so still
   Within the crib of Mary.

4. *Servant (2)*
   All shall come and bow the knee;
   Wise and happy their souls shall be,
   Loving such a divinity,
   As all may see
   In Jesus, Son of Mary.

5. *Servant (3)*
   Now is born Immanuel,
   Prophesied once by Ezekiel,
   Promised Mary by Gabriel—
   Ah, who can tell
   Thy praises, Son of Mary!

6. *Servant (4)*
   Thou my lazy heart hast stirred,
   Thou, the Father's eternal Word,
   Greater than aught that ear hath heard,
   Thou tiny bird
   Of love, thou Son of Mary.

7. *Servant (1)*
   Sweet and lovely little One,
   Thou princely, beautiful, God's own Son,
   Without Thee all of us were undone;
   Our love is won
   By Thine, O Son of Mary.

8. *Servant (2)*
   Little Man, and God indeed,
   Little and poor, Thou art all we need;
   We will follow where Thou dost lead,
   And we will heed
   Our Brother, born of Mary.

27. KING JESUS HATH A GARDEN

Dutch,
trans. G. R. Woodward

Dutch, (17th Century)
harm. Charles Wood

1. King Je - sus hath a gar - den, full of di - vers flow'rs,
2. The Li - ly, white in bloss - om there, is Chas - ti - ty;

Where
The

I go cul - ling pos - ies gay, all times and hours.
Vi - o - let, with sweet per - fume, Hu - mil - i - ty.

There

naught is heard But Par - a - dise bird, Harp, dul - ci - mer, lute, With

cym - bal, Trump and tym - bal, And the ten - der, sooth - ing flute; With

cym - bal, Trump and tym - bal, And the ten - der, sooth - ing flute.

Copyright, A.R. Mowbray & Co. Ltd., from The Cowley Carol Book

B.P. 103

3. The bonny Damask-rose is known as Patíence;
   The blithe and thrifty Marygold, Obedíence.
   There naught is heard, etc.

4. The Crown Imperial bloometh too in yonder place;
   'Tis Charity, of stock divine, the flower of grace.
   There naught is heard, etc.

5. Yet, mid the brave, the bravest prize of all may claim
   The Star of Bethlem – JESUS – blessèd be His Name!
   There naught is heard, etc.

6. Ah! Jesu Lord, my heal and weal, my bliss complete,
   Make Thou my heart Thy garden-plot, fair, trim and neat,
   That I may hear this musick clear:
   Harp, dulcimer, lute,
   With cymbal, Trump and tymbal,
   And the tender, soothing flute.

28. LITTLE JESUS, SWEETLY SLEEP
(ROCKING)

Czech,
trans. Percy Dearmer (1867-1936) *

Czech, arr. W.L.R.

Andante tranquillo

1. Lit - tle Je - sus, sweet - ly sleep, do not stir; We will lend a
2. Ma - ry's lit - tle ba - by, sleep, sweet - ly sleep, Sleep in com - fort,

coat of fur; We will rock you, rock you, rock you, We will rock you, rock you, rock you;
slum - ber deep; We will rock you, rock you, rock you, We will rock you, rock you, rock you;

See the fur to keep you warm, Snug - ly round your ti - ny form.
We will serve you all we can, Dar - ling, dar - ling lit - tle man.

* From the Oxford Book of Carols, by permission of The Oxford University Press

29. LOVE CAME DOWN AT CHRISTMAS

Christina Rossetti (1830-1894)

★ Sidney Hann

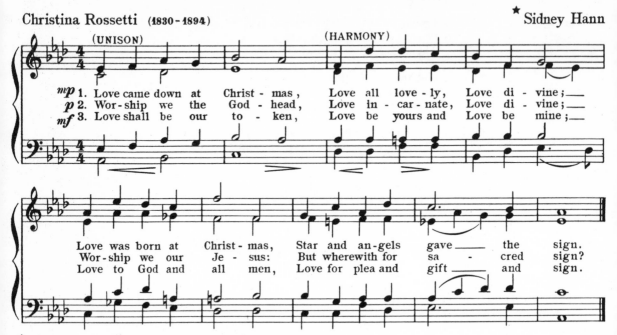

(UNISON)   (HARMONY)

mp 1. Love came down at Christ - mas, Love all love - ly, Love di - vine; ___
p 2. Wor - ship we the God - head, Love in - car - nate, Love di - vine; ___
mf 3. Love shall be our to - ken, Love be yours and Love be mine; ___

Love was born at Christ - mas, Star and an - gels gave ___ the sign.
Wor - ship we our Je - sus: But wherewith for sa - cred sign?
Love to God and all men, Love for plea and gift ___ and sign.

Copyright: Congregational Union of England and Wales

30. LULLAY, THOU LITTLE TINY CHILD
(THE COVENTRY CAROL)

Traditional

Traditional

Slow and expressive

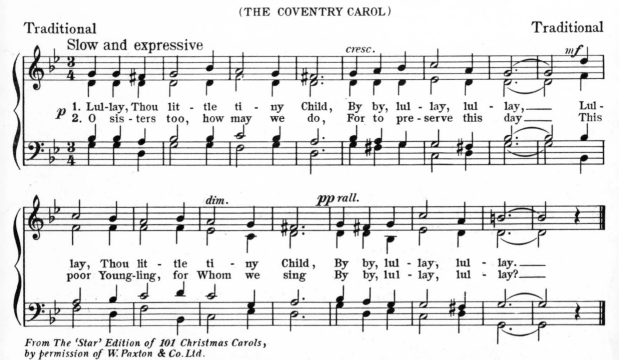

cresc.   *mf*

p 1. Lul - lay, Thou lit - tle ti - ny Child, By by, lul - lay, lul - lay, ___ Lul -
2. O sis - ters too, how may we do, For to pre - serve this day ___ This

dim.   *pp* rall.

lay, Thou lit - tle ti - ny Child, By by, lul - lay, lul - lay. ___
poor Young - ling, for Whom we sing By by, lul - lay, lul - lay? ___

From The 'Star' Edition of 101 Christmas Carols,
by permission of W. Paxton & Co. Ltd.

3. Herod the king in his raging
Chargèd he hath this day
His men of might, in his own sight,
All children young to slay.

4. Then woe is me, poor Child, for Thee!
And ever, morn and day,
For Thy parting nor say nor sing
By by, lullay, lullay.

31. MASTERS IN THIS HALL

William Morris (1834-1896)

French, arr. W. L. R.

Masters in this Hall, Hear ye news to-day Brought from o-ver-sea And

ev-er I you pray:—

Now-ell! Now-ell! Now-ell! Now-ell sing we clear! Holp-en
Now-ell! Now-ell! Now-ell! Now-ell sing we loud! God to-

are all folk on earth, Born is God's son so dear. cast a-down the proud.
day hath poor folk raised And

2. Then to Bethlem town
We went two and two
And in a sorry place
Heard the oxen low:

3. Therein did we see
A sweet and goodly may
And a little child
On her arm had she:

4. This is Christ the Lord,
Masters be ye glad!
Christmas is come in,
And no folk should be sad:

48

32. O COME, ALL YE FAITHFUL

Latin, trans. Frederick Oakeley (1802-1880)   J. Reading

1. O come, all ye faith - ful, Joy-ful and tri - um - phant, O
2. True God of True God, Light of Light e - ter - nal,

come ye, O come ye to Beth - le - hem; Come and be -
Lo!_ He ab - hors not the Vir - gin's womb; Son of the

hold Him, Born the King of an - gels: O come, let us a - dore Him, O
Fath - er, Be - got - ten not cre - a - ted: O come, let us a - dore Him, O

come, let us a - dore Him, O come, let us a - dore Him, Christ the Lord.

Omit chord in verses 2,3,4.

3.   Sing, choirs of angels,
        Sing in exultation,
   Sing, all ye citizens of heav'n above,
        Sing ye, "All glory
        To God in the highest."
      O come, let us adore Him,
      O come, let us adore Him,
   O come, let us adore Him, Christ the Lord.

4.   Yea, Lord, we greet Thee,
        Born this happy morning;
   Jesu, to Thee be glory given,
        Word of the Father,
        Now in flesh appearing:
      O come, let us adore Him,
      O come, let us adore Him,
   O come, let us adore Him, Christ the Lord.

33. O LEAVE YOUR SHEEP

Words translated from the French
(*"Quittez, Pasteurs"*) by Alice Raleigh

French Carol,
harm. & arr. C.H.Kitson

Moderato ♩=72

By permission of Novello & Co. Ltd.

B.P. 103

Lyrics:
2. You'll find Him laid —— With-in a sim-ple sta - ble,

A Babe new-born, —— In pov-er-ty for-lorn, —— In love ar-rayed, —— A love so deep,'tis a - ble To search the night for you, —— 'Tis He, 'tis He, 'Tis He, the Shep-herd true, 'Tis He, 'tis He, 'Tis He, the Shep-herd true.

Poco meno mosso

52

34. O LITTLE TOWN OF BETHLEHEM
(First Tune)

Phillips Brooks (1835-1893)   *Traditional, arr. R. Vaughan Williams

1. O lit-tle town of Beth-le-hem, How still we see thee lie! A-bove thy deep and dream-less sleep The si-lent stars go by. Yet in thy dark streets shin-eth The ev-er-last-ing light; The hopes and fears of all the years Are met in thee to-night.

2. O morn-ing stars, to-geth-er Pro-claim the ho-ly birth, And prais-es sing to God the King, And peace to men on earth; For Christ is born of Ma-ry, And, gath-ered all a-bove, While mor-tals sleep, the an-gels keep Their watch of won-d'ring love.

* From the Oxford Book of Carols, by permission of The Oxford University Press

3. How silently, how silently
   The wondrous gift is given!
So God imparts to human hearts
   The blessings of His heav'n.
No ear may hear His coming;
   But in this world of sin,
Where meek souls will receive Him, still
   The dear Christ enters in.

4. O Holy Child of Bethlehem,
   Descend to us, we pray;
Cast out our sin, and enter in,
   Be born in us today.
We hear the Christmas angels
   The great glad tidings tell.
O come to us, abide with us,
   Our Lord Immanuel.

35. O LITTLE TOWN OF BETHLEHEM

(Second Tune)

Phillips Brooks (1835-1893)   *Lewis H. Redner

mp

1. O lit-tle town of Beth-le-hem, How still we see thee lie! A-
2. O morn-ing stars, to - geth - er Pro-claim the ho - ly birth, And

bove thy deep and dream-less sleep The si - lent stars go by. Yet
prais-es sing to God the King, And peace to men on earth; For

in thy dark streets shin - eth The ev - er - last - ing light; The
Christ is born of Ma - ry, And, gath-ered all a - bove, While

hopes and fears of all the years Are met in thee to - night.
mor-tals sleep, the an - gels keep Their watch of won - d'ring love.

3. How silently, how silently
    The wondrous gift is given!
So God imparts to human hearts
    The blessings of His heav'n.
No ear may hear His coming;
    But in this world of sin,
Where meek souls will receive Him, still
    The dear Christ enters in.

4. O Holy Child of Bethlehem,
    Descend to us, we pray;
Cast out our sin, and enter in,
    Be born in us today.
We hear the Christmas angels
    The great glad tidings tell.
O come to us, abide with us,
    Our Lord Immanuel.

36. O MORTAL MAN, REMEMBER WELL
(SUSSEX MUMMERS' CAROL)

Traditional*   Traditional, arr. W. L. R.

1. O mor-tal man, re - mem - ber well, When Christ our Lord was born, He was cru-ci-fied be - tween two thieves, And crown-èd with the thorn, And crown - èd with the thorn.
2. O mor-tal man, re - mem - ber well, When Christ died on the rood, 'Twas for our sins and wick-ed ways Christ shed His prec-ious blood, Christ shed His prec - ious blood.

*From Lucy E. Broadwood's English Traditional Songs and Carols, by permission of Boosey & Hawkes Ltd.

3. O mortal man, remember well,
   When Christ was wrapped in clay,
   He was taken to a sepulchre
   Where no man ever lay.

4. God bless the mistress of this house
   With gold chain round her breast;
   Where e'er her body sleeps or wakes,
   Lord, send her soul to rest.

5. God bless the master of this house
   With happiness beside;
   Where e'er his body rides or walks
   Lord Jesus be his guide.

6. God bless your house, your children too,
   Your cattle and your store;
   The Lord increase you day by day,
   And send you more and more.

37. ONCE IN ROYAL DAVID'S CITY

Cecil Frances Alexander (1823-1895)   H. J. Gauntlett (1805-1876)

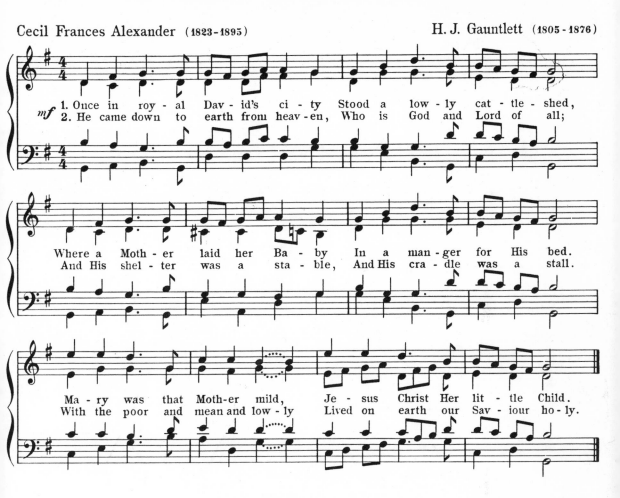

1. Once in roy - al Dav - id's ci - ty Stood a low - ly cat - tle - shed,
2. He came down to earth from heav - en, Who is God and Lord of all;

Where a Moth - er laid her Ba - by In a man - ger for His bed.
And His shel - ter was a sta - ble, And His cra - dle was a stall.

Ma - ry was that Moth - er mild, Je - sus Christ Her lit - tle Child.
With the poor and mean and low - ly Lived on earth our Sav - iour ho - ly.

3. And through all His wondrous childhood
   He would honour and obey,
   Love and watch the lowly Mother
   In Whose gentle arms He lay.
   Christian children all must be
   Mild, obedient, good as He.

4. For He is our childhood's Pattern,
   Day by day like us He grew;
   He was little, weak and helpless,
   Tears and smiles like us He knew;
   And He feeleth for our sadness,
   And He shareth in our gladness.

5. And our eyes at last shall see Him,
   Through His own redeeming love,
   For that Child so dear and gentle
   Is our Lord in heaven above;
   And He leads His children on
   To the place where He is gone.

38. ON CHRISTMAS NIGHT ALL CHRISTIANS SING

Traditional*

Traditional, arr. W.L.R.

1. On Christ-mas night all
2. Then why should men on
3. When sin de-parts be-

Christ - ians sing, To hear the news the an - gels bring. On
earth be so sad, Since our Re - deem - er made us glad, Then
fore— His grace, Then life and health come in its place, When

Christ - mas night all Christ - ians sing, To hear the news the
why should men on earth be so sad, Since our Re - deem - er
sin de - parts be - fore— His grace, Then life and health come

an - gels bring— News of great joy, news of great mirth,—
made us glad; When from our sin He set us free,—
in its place. An - gels and men with joy may sing,—

*By permission of the International Folk Music Council

News of our mer-ci-ful King's birth. ____
All for to gain our lib-er-ty. ____
All for to see the new-born King. ____

4. *f* All out of dark-ness we have light, Which

made the an-gels sing this night, *p* All out of dark-ness we have light, Which

made the an-gels sing this night: *f* Glo-ry to God and peace to men, ____

Now and for ev-er-more, A-men. ____

39. PAST THREE A CLOCK

G. R. Woodward

'London Waits,'
harm. Charles Wood

From the Cambridge Carol Book, by permission of the S.P.C.K.

3. Mid earth rejoices
    Hearing such voices
    Ne'ertofore só well
    Carolling *Nowell*.

4. Hinds o'er the pearly
    Dewy lawn early
    Seek the high Stranger
    Laid in the manger.

5. Cheese from the dairy
    Bring they for Mary,
    And, not for money,
    Butter and honey.

6. Light out of star-land
    Leadeth from far land
    Princes, to meet Him,
    Worship and greet Him.

7. Myrrh from full coffer,
    Incense they offer;
    Nor is the golden
    Nugget withholden.

8. Thus they: I pray you,
    Up, sirs, nor stay you
    Till ye confess Him
    Likewise, and bless Him.

40. PRAISE TO GOD IN THE HIGHEST

Russian, trans. A. F. D.*

Russian, arr. W. L. R.

1. Praise to God in the high - est! Bless us, O
3. May the truth in its beau - ty flour - ish tri -
5. May the good be o - beyed, and e - vil be

Fa - ther! **ff** PRAISE TO THEE. 2. Guide and
um - phant: PRAISE TO THEE. 4. May the
con - quered: PRAISE TO THEE. 6. Give us

pros - per the na - tions, rul - ers and peo - ple:
mills bring us bread, for food and for giv - ing:
laugh - ter, and set us gai - ly re - joic - ing:

ff PRAISE TO THEE. 7. Peace on earth, and good -

will be ev - er a - mong us: **ff** PRAISE TO THEE.

* From the Oxford Book of Carols, by permission of The Oxford University Press

41. SEE, AMID THE WINTER'S SNOW

Edward Caswall (1814-1878)

John Goss (1800-1880)

(SOLO or UNISON)

1. See, a-mid the win-ter's snow, Born for us on earth be-low,
2. Lo, with-in a man-ger lies He Who built the star-ry skies,

See, the Lamb of God ap-pears, Promised from e-ter-nal years.
He Who, throned in height sub-lime, Sits a-mid the cher-u-bim.

CHORUS (Harmony)

Hail, thou ev-er-bless-èd morn! Hail, re-demp-tion's hap-py dawn!

Sing through all Je-ru-sa-lem: Christ is born in Beth-le-hem!

3. Say, ye holy shepherds, say
What your joyful news today;
Wherefore have ye left your sheep
On the lonely mountain steep?

4. As we watched at dead of night,
Lo, we saw a wondrous light:
Angels, singing peace on earth,
Told us of the Saviour's birth.

5. Sacred Infant, all divine,
What a tender love was Thine,
Thus to come from highest bliss
Down to such a world as this!

6. Teach, O teach us, holy Child,
By Thy face so meek and mild,
Teach us to resemble Thee
In Thy sweet humility.

42. SILENT NIGHT, HOLY NIGHT

Joseph Mohr (1792-1848)

Franz Gruber (1787-1863)
arr. W.L.R.

1. Si - lent night, ho - ly night! All is calm, all is bright Round yon Vir - gin Moth - er and Child. Ho - ly In - fant so ten - der and mild, Sleep in heav - en - ly peace, _____ Sleep _____ in heav - en - ly peace. _____

2. Si - lent night, ho - ly night! Shep - herds first saw the light, Heard re - sound - ing clear _____ and long, Far and near, _____ the an - gel song: Christ the Sa - viour is here, _____ Christ _____ the Sa - viour is here. _____

3. Si - lent night, ho - ly night! Son of God, oh how bright Love is smil - ing from _____ Thy face! Peals for us _____ the hour _____ of grace. Christ our Sa - viour is born, _____ Christ _____ our Sa - viour is born. _____

43. SWEET WAS THE SONG THE VIRGIN SANG
(LUTE-BOOK LULLABY)

Andante
molto espress.

17th Century, arr. H.A.C.

Sweet was the song the Vir-gin sang When She to Beth-lem Ju - da

When She to Beth-lem Ju - da

came And was de-liv-ered of a Son, That blessèd Je-sus hath to name:

"Lul-la, lul-la, lul-la, lul-la-by, Lul-la, lul-la, lul-la, lul-la-by. Sweet Babe,"___ sang

She, "my Son, And eke a Sa-viour born, Who hast vouch-saf-èd from on high To

To vis-it
vis - it us that were for - lorn: La-lu-la, la - lu-la, la - lu - la -

rall.

-by, Sweet Babe," sang She, And rocked Him sweet - ly on Her knee.

44. THE BOAR'S HEAD IN HAND BEAR I
(BOAR'S HEAD CAROL)

Traditional
Rather slowly

Traditional, arr. H.A.C.

(SOLO or UNISON)

1. The boar's head in hand bear I, Be-decked with bays and rose - ma - ry; And I

Verses 2 & 3

2. The boar's head, as I un-der-stand, Is the rar-est dish in all the land, Which
3. Our stew-ard hath pro-vi-ded this In hon-our of the King of bliss, Which

pray you, my mas-ters, be mer-ry, Quot es - tis in con-vi-vi-o.

thus be-decked with a gay gar-land, Let us ser-vi-re can-ti-co.
on this day to be serv-èd is In Re-gi-nen-si a-tri-o.

CHORUS (Harmony) after each Verse

Ca - put a - pri de - fe - ro, Red - dens lau - des Do - mi - no.

B.P. 103

45. THE FIRST DAY OF CHRISTMAS

Traditional
Gaily

Traditional, arr. W. L. R.†

1. The first day of Christ-mas my true love sent to me A part-ridge in a pear tree.— 2. The sec-ond day of Christ-mas my true love sent to me Two tur-tle-doves and a part-ridge in a pear tree.—

3. The third day of Christ-mas my true love sent to me Three French hens,

(last time rall.)

two tur-tle-doves and a part-ridge in a pear tree.—

D.S.

† *This arrangement of the better known tune for this carol is substituted for the one which appeared in the earlier editions of this book. W.L.R.*

* *This bar is sung twice in verse 4, three times in verse 5, and so on.*

4. The fourth day — Four calling birds, three French hens, etc.
5. The fifth day — Five gold rings, four calling birds, etc.
6. The sixth day — Six geese a-laying, five gold rings, etc.
7. The seventh day — Seven swans a-swimming, six geese a-laying, etc.
8. The eighth day — Eight maids a-milking, seven swans a-swimming, etc.
9. The ninth day — Nine ladies dancing, eight maids a-milking, etc.
10. The tenth day — Ten lords a-leaping, nine ladies dancing, etc.
11. The eleventh day — Eleven pipers piping, ten lords a-leaping, etc.
12. The twelfth day — Twelve drummers drumming, eleven pipers piping, etc.

46. THE FIRST GOOD JOY THAT MARY HAD

(THE SEVEN JOYS OF MARY)

Traditional

Traditional, arr. H.A.C.

Allegretto

1. The first good joy that Mary had, It was the joy of one; _____ To
2. The next good joy that Mary had, It was the joy of two; _____ To

see the bless - èd Je - sus Christ When He was first Her Son. _____
see Her own Son Je - sus Christ Mak - ing the lame to go. _____

When He was first Her Son, Good Lord; And hap - py may we be; _____ Praise
Mak - ing the lame to go, Good Lord; And hap - py may we be; _____ Praise

Fa - ther, Son and Ho - ly Ghost To all e - ter - ni - ty. _____

3. The next good joy that Mary had,
   It was the joy of three;
   To see Her own Son Jesus Christ
   Making the blind to see.
   Making the blind to see, Good Lord;

4. The next good joy that Mary had,
   It was the joy of four;
   To see Her own Son Jesus Christ
   Reading the Bible o'er.
   Reading the Bible o'er, Good Lord;

5. The next good joy that Mary had,
   It was the joy of five;
   To see Her own Son Jesus Christ
   Raising the dead to life.
   Raising the dead to life, Good Lord;

6. The next good joy that Mary had,
   It was the joy of six;
   To see Her own Son Jesus Christ
   Upon the Crucifix.
   Upon the Crucifix, Good Lord;

7. The next good joy that Mary had,
   It was the joy of seven;
   To see Her own Son Jesus Christ
   Ascending into heaven.
   Ascending into heaven, Good Lord;

B. P. 103

66

47. THE FIRST NOWELL

Traditional   Traditional

mf 1. The first Now-ell the an-gel did say Was to cer-tain poor
2. They look-èd up and saw a star Shin-ing in the

shepherds in fields as they lay; *p* In fields where they lay, keep-ing their
east, be-yond them far, And to the earth it gave great

CHORUS

sheep, On a cold win-ter's night that was so deep: *f* Now-ell, Now-
light, And so it con-tin-ued both day and night:

ell, Now-ell, Now-ell, Born is the King of Is-ra-el!

3. And by the light of that same star,
   Three wise men came from country far;
   To seek for a King was their intent,
   And to follow the star wherever it went:

4. This star drew nigh to the north-west,
   O'er Bethlehem it took its rest,
   And there it did both stop and stay
   Right over the place where Jesus lay:

5. Then entered in those wise men three
   Full reverently upon their knee,
   And offered there in His presence
   Their gold and myrrh and frankincense:

6. Then let us all with one accord
   Sing praises to our heav'nly Lord,
   That hath made heav'n and earth of nought,
   And with His blood mankind hath bought:

B.P. 103

48. THE HOLLY AND THE IVY

Traditional
Moderato

★ Traditional, arr. H.A.C.
(Collected by C.J. Sharp)

1. The hol-ly and the i - vy, When they are both full - grown, Of
2. The hol-ly bears a blos - som As white as li - ly flower; And

all the trees that are in the wood, The hol - ly bears the crown.
Ma - ry bore sweet Je - sus Christ To be our sweet Sa - viour.

CHORUS (Harmony)

O the ris-ing of the sun, — And the running of the deer, The

play-ing of the mer-ry or - gan, Sweet sing-ing in the choir.

*By permission of Novello & Co. Ltd.

3. The holly bears a berry
   As red as any blood;
   And Mary bore sweet Jesus Christ
   To do poor sinners good.

4. The holly bears a prickle
   As sharp as any thorn;
   And Mary bore sweet Jesus Christ
   On Christmas Day in the morn.

5. The holly bears a bark
   As bitter as any gall;
   And Mary bore sweet Jesus Christ
   For to redeem us all.

6. The holly and the ivy,
   When they are both full-grown,
   Of all the trees that are in the wood,
   The holly bears the crown.

49. THE MOON SHINES BRIGHT

Traditional   Traditional

1. The moon shines bright and the stars give light A lit-tle be-fore the day, Our might-y Lord He looked on us, And bade us wake and pray.
2. A-wake, a-wake, good peo-ple all, A-wake, and you shall hear, The Lord our God died on the cross, For us He loved so dear.

From The "Star" Edition of 101 Christmas Carols, by permission of W. Paxton & Co. Ltd.

3. And for the saving of our souls
   Christ died upon the cross,
   We ne'er can show for Jesus Christ
   The love He showed for us.

4. My song is done, I must be gone,
   I stay no longer here;
   God bless you all, both great and small,
   And send you a glad new year!

50. THE OLD YEAR NOW AWAY IS FLED
(GREENSLEEVES)

Traditional   Traditional, arr. H.A.C.
Moderato

1. The old year now a-way is fled, The new year now is en-ter-èd; Then let us now our sins down-tread, And joy-ful-ly all ap-pear.
2. And now with new-year's gifts each friend Un-to each oth-er they do send; God grant we may our lives a-mend, And that the truth may ap-pear.

Mer - ry be＿ the hol - i - day,＿ And let us run＿ with sport and play,
Like the snake cast off your skin＿ Of e - vil thoughts and wick - ed sin,

Hang＿ sor - row, cast care a - way,＿ God send you a hap - py new year!＿
To a - mend this new year be - gin,＿ God send us a mer - ry new year!＿

51. THIS IS THE TRUTH SENT FROM ABOVE

Traditional*

Traditional, arr. W. L. R.

1. This is the truth sent from a - bove, The truth of God, the God of love, There-
2. The first thing which I do re - late Is that God did man cre - ate; The

p (Hum)

fore don't turn me＿ from your door, But heark - en all＿ both rich and poor.
next thing which to ＿ you I'll tell – Wo - man was made with man to dwell.

* By permission of Stainer & Bell Ltd.

70

3. And we were heirs to endless woes, Till God the Lord did in-ter-pose; And
4. And at that sea-son of the year Our blest Re-deem-er did ap-pear; He

so a pro - mise soon did run That He would re - deem us by His Son.
here did live, and here did preach, And ma - ny thou - sands He did teach.

5. Thus He in love to us be-haved, To show us how we must be saved; And

if you want to know the way, Be pleased to hear what He did say.

52. UNTO US A BOY IS BORN

15th century German,
trans. Percy Dearmer (1867-1936)*

German, arr. W.L.R.

f 1. Un-to us a Boy is born, King of all cre-a-tion, Came He to a

world for-lorn, The Lord of ev-'ry na - - - - - - - tion.

Women's Voices

p

Piano

p

2. Cradled in a stall was He With sleep-y cows and ass-es; But the ve-ry

beasts could see That He all men sur-pass - - - - - - es.

* From the Oxford Book of Carols, by permission of The Oxford University Press

Men's Voices

3. He-rod then with fear was filled: 'A prince', he said, 'in Jew-ry!' All the lit-tle boys he killed At Beth-lem in his fu - - - - - - ry.

Women's Voices

4. Now may Ma-ry's Son, Who came So long a-go to love us, Lead us all with hearts a-flame Un-to the joys a-bove _____ us.

53. WASSAIL, WASSAIL, ALL OVER THE TOWN!
(GLOUCESTERSHIRE WASSAIL)

Traditional*

With vigour

Descant *(Verses 2 & 4)*

Traditional, arr. W. L. R.

1. Was - sail,— Was - sail,— all o - ver the town! Our toast it is
2. So here is to Cher - ry and to his right cheek, Pray God send our

white, and our ale it is brown, Our bowl it is made of the
mas - ter a good piece of beef, And a good piece of beef that

white ma - ple tree ;— With the was - sail - ing bowl we'll drink— to thee.
may we all see ;— With the was - sail - ing bowl we'll drink— to thee.

* From the Oxford Book of Carols, by permission of The Oxford University Press

3. And here is to Dobbin and to his right eye,
   Pray God send our master a good Christmas pie,
   And a good Christmas pie that may we all see;
   With our wassailing bowl we'll drink to thee.

4. So here is to Broad May and to her broad horn,
   May God send our master a good crop of corn,
   And a good crop of corn that may we all see;
   With the wassailing bowl we'll drink to thee.

5. And here is to Fillpail and to her left ear.
   Pray God send our master a happy New Year,
   And a happy New Year as e'er he did see;
   With our wassailing bowl we'll drink to thee.

54. WE THREE KINGS OF ORIENT ARE

J.H.Hopkins (1820-1891)
arr. H.A.C.

Moderato

SOLO *(Male Trio in Verses 1 & 5)*

1. We three kings of O - rient are; Bear-ing gifts we tra-verse a -
far Field and foun - tain, moor and moun-tain, Fol-low-ing yon - der star.

CHORUS *(Harmony)*

O ___ star of won - der, star of night, Star with roy - al beau-ty bright,
West-ward lead - ing, still pro-ceed - ing, Guide us to thy per - fect light.

Melchior
2. Born a King on Bethlehem's plain,
Gold I bring, to crown Him again,
King for ever, ceasing never
Over us all to reign.

Gaspar
3. Frankincense to offer have I,
Incense owns a Deity nigh.
Prayer and praising, all men raising
Worship Him, God most high.

Balthazar
4. Myrrh is mine, its bitter perfume
Breathes a life of gathering gloom;
Sorrowing, sighing, bleeding, dying,
Sealed in the stone-cold tomb.

5. Glorious now behold Him arise,
King and God and sacrifice!
Heav'n sings Alleluia,
Alleluia the earth replies.

55. WHENCE IS THAT GOODLY FRAGRANCE?

(Quelle est cette odeur agréable?)

Trans. A. B. Ramsay *

Old French Carol
arr. W. L. R.†

1. Whence is that good-ly fragrance flowing, Stealing our sens-es all a - way? Nev-er the like did come a - blow-ing, Shepherds, from flow-'ry fields in May. Whence is that good-ly fragrance flow-ing, Stealing our sens-es all a - way?

Quelle est cette o-deur a-gré-a-ble, Bergers, qui ra-vit tous nos sens? S'ex-ha-le-t'il rien de sem-bla-ble Au mi-lieu des fleurs du printemps! Quelle est cette o-deur a-gré-a-ble, Bergers, qui ra-vit tous nos sens?

*By permission of the translator. †This carol may be sung by a solo voice.

B.P. 103

S A

p 3. Beth - le - hem! there in man - ger ly - ing Find your Re - deem - er, haste a -
*A Beth - lé - em dans u - ne crê - che Il vient de vous naître un Sau -

T B

molto cresc.

f

way! Run ye with eag - er foot-steps hie - ing! Wor-ship the
veur. Al - lons que rien ne vous em - pê - che D'a - do - rer

molto cresc.

f

p sub.

Sa - viour born to - day! Beth - le - hem! there in man - ger ly - ing
vo - tre Ré - demp-teur. *A Beth - lé - em dans u - ne crê - che

p sub.

*When sung in French this bar should have the rhythm ♩ ♩ ♩

poco rit.   pp

Find your Re - deem - er, haste a - way!
Il vient de vous naître un Sau - veur.

56. WHILE SHEPHERDS WATCHED THEIR FLOCKS BY NIGHT

Nahum Tate (1652-1715)   Ravenscroft

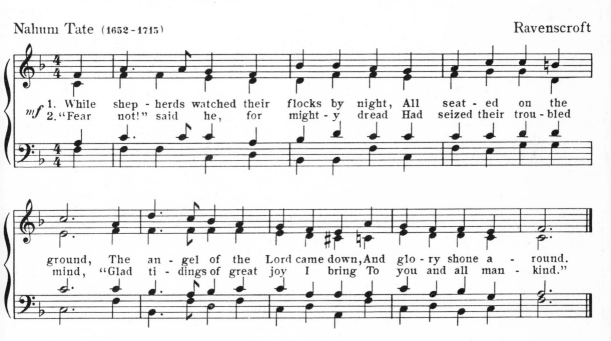

1. While shep - herds watched their flocks by night, All seat - ed on the
2. "Fear not!" said he, for might - y dread Had seized their trou - bled

ground, The an - gel of the Lord came down, And glo - ry shone a - round.
mind, "Glad ti - dings of great joy I bring To you and all man - kind."

3. "To you, in David's town, this day
    Is born, of David's line,
  A Saviour, Who is Christ the Lord;
    And this shall be the sign:

4. "The heavenly Babe you there shall find
    To human view displayed,
  All meanly wrapped in swaddling bands
    And in a manger laid."

5. Thus spake the seraph; and forthwith
    Appeared a shining throng
  Of angels, praising God, and thus
    Addressed their joyful song:

6. "All glory be to God on high,
    And to the earth be peace;
  Goodwill henceforth from heaven to men
    Begin, and never cease!"

57. WILLIE, TAKE YOUR LITTLE DRUM
(PATAPAN)

La Monnoye
trans. Percy Dearmer (1867–1936)

Burgundian Carol,
arr. Martin Shaw

Tu - re - lu, tu - re - lu, tu - re - lu, tu - re - lu, tu - re -

Verse 2

2. Thus the men of old - en days Loved the King of

Pat - a - pan, pat - a - pan, pat - a - pan, pat - a - pan, pat - a -

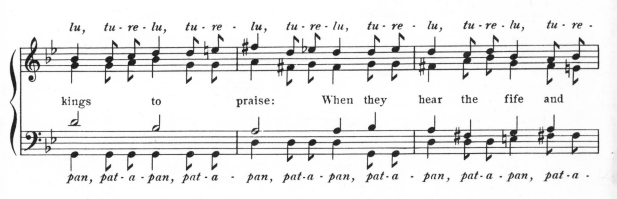

lu, tu - re - lu, tu - re - lu, tu - re - lu, tu - re - lu, tu - re - lu, tu - re -

kings to praise: When they hear the fife and

pan, pat - a - pan, pat - a - pan, pat - a - pan, pat - a - pan, pat - a -

lu, tu - re - lu, tu - re - lu, tu - re - lu, lu, lu, tu - re - lu, lu,

drum, Tu - re - lu - re - lu, pat - a - pat - a - pan, When they

pan, pat - a - pan, pat - a - pan, pat - a - pan, pat - a - pan, pat - a - pan, pat - a -

lu, tu - re - lu, tu - re - lu, tu - re - lu, tu - re - lu, tu - re - lu, tu - re - lu.

hear the fife and drum, Sure our chil - dren won't be dumb!

D.C.

pan, pat - a - pan, pat - a - pan, pat - a - pan, pat - a - pan, pat - a - pan, pan, pan.

MODERN COMPOSITIONS

To my Mother

58. A SPOTLESS ROSE

(CAROL-ANTHEM)

(For use at Christmastide)

Words of
14th Century origin

Herbert Howells

With easeful movement

Soprano

p

A Spot-less Rose⏤ is blow⏤ ing, Sprung from a ten -

Alto

p

A Spot-less Rose is⏤ blow - ing, Sprung from a ten -

Tenor

p

A Spot-less Rose⏤ is blow⏤ ing, Sprung from a ten -

Bass

p

A Spot-less Rose⏤ is blow⏤ ing, Sprung from a ten -

Piano
(for practice only)

p

mp

- der root,⏤ Of ancient seers'⏤ fore-show-ing, Of Jes-se pro-mised

mp

- der root,⏤ Of ancient seers'⏤ fore-show-ing, Of Jes-se pro-mised

mp

- der root,⏤ Of ancient seers'⏤ fore-show-ing, Of Jes-se pro-mised

mp

- der root,⏤ Of ancient seers'⏤ fore-show-ing, Of Jes-se pro-mised

mp

83

B.P. 103

59. BALULALOW
(A CRADLE SONG)

Author unknown (16th - 17th century)

Peter Warlock

60. CAUX CAROL

Morris Martin

Paul Petrocokino

1. Sheep nor shep-herds, none are here, High up-on the moun-tain,
2. Stars look down from heav-en's ring, High a-bove the moun-tain,

Yet our watch-ful lights ap-pear, Shin-ing on the moun-tain;
And the an-gel voic-es sing All a-round the moun-tain;

Christ _____ the Lord _____ is born this Christ-mas morn - ing,
Christ _____ the Lord _____ is born this Christ-mas morn - ing,

Snow and sun His prais-es sing, Born this Christ-mas morn - ing.
O ye na-tions, prais-es sing, Born this Christ-mas morn - ing.

3. Dark the trees like man-kind's sin, High up-on the moun - tain,

White as grace the snow draws in, Cov - 'ring all the moun - tain;

Christ ———— the Lord ———— is born this Christ-mas morn - ing,

Soon the world shall hail its King, Born this Christ-mas morn - ing.

61. CHRISTMAS CRADLE SONG

John Morrison

Marie Joy Sanger

1. Still and dark the night a-bout the sheil-ing,
2. Still and dark the night a-bout the man-ger,

Clear and cold the light from shin-ing star.
Clear and cold the light from God's bright star.

Si-lent are the flocks, the bells are
Si-lent were the flocks when, for this

peal - ing
Stran - ger,

Ev'-ning time so faint-ly from a - far.
An-gels sang His glo-ry from a - far.

pp
ten.
Hush thee, lit - tle one, Day-spring now is done. Hush thee, do not weep,
Hush thee, lit - tle one, Bless - èd Ma - ry's Son Guard thee, guide, and keep
pp sub.
ten.
poco rit.
p a tempo
Cra - dled safe - ly, sleep. Once on such an eve a Mo - ther
Lit - tle ones who sleep. For on such an eve the Christ Child
p a tempo
poco rit.
come prima
ho - ly Rocked the Son of God in man - ger
low - ly Came to us, that we might serve Him
pp
p
1
2
low - ly.
whol - ly.
smorz.
smorz.
ppp

62. CHRISTMAS IS COMING

Old Rhyme

H. Walford Davies

Christ-mas is com-ing, the geese are getting fat, Please to put a pen-ny in the

fat,

old man's hat. old man's hat. _____ If you

have-n't got a penny, a ha'-p'ny 'll do, a ha'-p'ny 'll do, a ha'- p'ny 'll do,

pp ad lib. *cresc.*

two, _____ three, four!
four!

But a penny's bet-ter, A pen-ny or two are bet-ter, or three! or four!

ff a tempo

Christ-mas is com-ing, the geese are get-ting fat, Please to put a pen-ny in the

fat,

By permission of the Executors of Sir Walford Davies

63. COWBOY CAROL

Words and Music by Cecil Broadhurst
arr. Frances Roots Hadden

There'll be a new world be-gin-nin' from t'-night!

There'll be a new world be-gin-nin' from t'-night! _____

When I climb up to my sad-dle Gonna take Him to my

heart! There'll be a new world be-gin-nin' from t'-night! _____

SOLO Yay! Yip-pee! We're gon-na ride the trail!

Yay! Yip-pee! We're gon-na ride to day! When I

Solo climb up to my sad-dle Gon-na take Him to my heart! There'll be a

S A (Hum)

T B (Hum)

64. FARMERS' CAROL

Edward Devlin

Paul Petrocokino

WOMEN'S VOICES

O lit - tle King, in sta - ble born,____ O lit - tle Star, come
Heal-er of na - tions, born__ to pain,____ O Prince of Peace, or -

down from heav'n, O song of lark on snow - y
dained to bat - tle, O Lord of Death and spring - ing

morn,____ O lit - tle Lamb, to shep - herds giv - en.
grain,____ O King of kings, a - mong the cat - tle.

MIXED VOICES

Bread of the hun - gry na - tions, here are we____ To
Live in our hearts, and use our hands to feed____ The

sow, to reap, to toil____ for Thee.
starv - ing na - tions in____ their need.____

To G. K. Chesterton Esq.

65. HERE IS THE LITTLE DOOR
A CAROL-ANTHEM

Frances Chesterton

Herbert Howells

Soprano: Here is the lit-tle door, — lift up the latch, oh lift! We need not wan - der more but en-ter with our gift; — Our gift of fin-est gold,

Alto: Here is the lit-tle door, — lift up the latch, oh lift! We need not wan - der more but en-ter with our gift; — Our gift of fin-est gold,

Tenor: Here is the lit-tle door, — lift up the latch, oh lift! We need not wan - der more but en-ter with our gift; — Our gift of fin-est gold,

Bass: Here is the lit-tle door, — lift up the latch, oh lift! We need not wander more but en-ter with our gift; — Our gift of fin-est gold,

Gold that was nev-er bought nor sold; Myrrh to be strewn a-bout His Bed;—

Gold that was nev-er bought nor sold; Myrrh to be strewn a-bout His Bed;—

Gold that was nev-er bought nor sold; Myrrh to be strewn a-bout His Bed;—

Gold that was nev-er bought nor sold; Myrrh to be strewn a-bout His Bed;—

Poco meno mosso

In-cense in clouds a-bout His Head;— All for the Child that stirs not in His

In-cense in clouds a - bout His Head;— All for the Child that stirs not in His

In-cense in clouds a - bout His Head;— All for the Child that stirs not in His

In-cense in clouds a - bout His Head;— All for the Child that stirs not in His

Poco meno mosso

sleep, But ho - ly slum - - ber — holds with ass and sheep.

sleep, But ho - ly slum - - ber — holds with ass and — sheep.

sleep, But ho - ly slum - - ber — holds with ass and — sheep.

sleep, But ho - ly slum - ber holds with ass and — sheep.

Tempo primo

Bend low a - bout His Bed, ——— for each He has a gift; See how His

Bend low a - bout His Bed, ——— for each He has a gift; See how His

Bend low a - bout His Bed, ——— for each He has a gift; See how His

Bend low a - bout His Bed, ——— for each He has a gift; See how His

Tempo primo

Più tranquillo — rit. — Tempo primo

Myrrh for the hon-oured hap-py dead; — Gifts for His chil-dren, ter-ri-ble and

Myrrh for the hon-oured hap-py dead; — Gifts for His chil-dren, ter-ri-ble and

Myrrh for the hon-oured hap-py dead; — Gifts for His chil-dren, ter-ri-ble and

Myrrh for the hon-oured hap-py dead; — Gifts for His chil-dren, ter-ri-ble and

Più tranquillo — Tempo primo

Meno mosso

sweet, — Touched by such ti - ny hands and Oh such ti - ny feet. —

sweet, Touched by such ti - ny hands and Oh — such ti - ny feet. —

sweet, Touched by such ti - ny hands and Oh such ti - ny feet. —

sweet, Touched by such hands — and Oh — such feet. —

Meno mosso

66. IN THE BLEAK MID-WINTER

Christina Rossetti (1830-1894)

Gustav Holst* (1874-1934)

In moderate time

1. In the bleak mid-win-ter Frost-y wind made moan,— Earth stood hard as ir-on, Wa-ter like a stone; Snow had fal-len, snow on snow, Snow on snow, In the bleak mid-win-ter, Long a-go.

By permission of the Trustee of the late Gustav Holst

The metre of this hymn is irregular. The music as printed is that of the first verse, and it can easily be adapted to the others. Verses 2 & 3 run:—

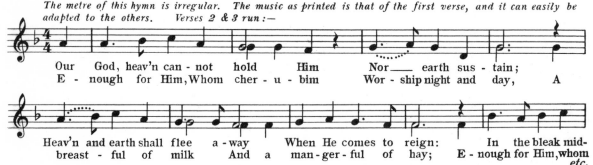

Our God, heav'n can-not hold Him Nor___ earth sus-tain;
E-nough for Him,Whom cher-u-bim Wor-ship night and day, A

Heav'n and earth shall flee a-way When He comes to reign: In the bleak mid-
breast-ful of milk And a man-ger-ful of hay; E-nough for Him,whom
etc.

2. Our God, heav'n cannot hold Him
   Nor earth sustain;
   Heav'n and earth shall flee away
   When He comes to reign:
   In the bleak mid-winter
   A stable-place sufficed
   The Lord God Almighty,
   Jesus Christ.

3. Enough for Him, Whom cherubim
   Worship night and day,
   A breastful of milk
   And a mangerful of hay;
   Enough for Him, Whom angels
   Fall down before,
   The ox and ass and camel
   Which adore.

4. Angels and archangels
   May have gathered there,
   Cherubim and seraphim
   Thronged the air:
   But only His Mother
   In Her maiden bliss
   Worshipped the Belovèd
   With a kiss.

5. What can I give Him,
   Poor as I am?
   If I were a shepherd
   I would bring a lamb;
   If I were a wise man
   I would do my part;
   Yet what I can I give Him —
   Give my heart.

67. LULLAY MY LIKING

Traditional
Allegretto

Gustav Holst*(1874-1934)

CHORUS

Lul - lay my lik - ing, my dear son, my sweet - ing;

Lul - lay my dear heart, mine own dear dar - ling!

SOLO

1. I saw a fair Maid - en Sit - ten and sing: She
lul - lèd a lit - tle Child, A swee - té Lord - ing:

CHORUS

Lul - lay my lik - ing, my dear son, my sweet - ing;

Lul - lay my dear heart, mine own dear dar - ling!

SOLO

2. That e - ter - nal Lord is He That made al - lé thing; Of
al - lé lord - és He is Lord, Of al - lé king - és King:

* By permission, from Curwen Edition No. 80589, published by
J. Curwen & Sons Ltd., 24, Berners St., London, W.1.

CHORUS

Lul - lay my lik - ing, my dear son, my sweet - ing;

Lul - lay my dear heart, mine own dear dar - ling!

SOLO

3. There was mic - kle mel - o - dy At that Child - és birth: Al - though they were in heav - en's bliss They ma - dé mic - kle mirth:

CHORUS

Lul - lay my lik - ing, my dear son, my sweet - ing;

Lul - lay my dear heart, mine own dear dar - ling!

CHORUS

4. An - gels bright they sang that night And said - én to that Child: 'Bless - èd be

Thou, and so be She That is both meek and mild':

Lul - lay my lik - ing, my dear son, my sweet - ing;

Lul - lay my dear heart, mine own dear dar - ling!

SOLO

5. Pray we now to that Child, And to His Moth - er dear, God grant them all His bless - ing That now mak - én cheer:

CHORUS

Lul - lay my lik - ing, my dear son, my sweet - ing;

Lul - lay my dear heart, mine own dear dar - ling!

68. MYN LYKING

Traditional

R. R. Terry*

69. O LITTLE TOWN OF BETHLEHEM
(Third Tune)

Phillips Brooks (1835-1893)　　　　　　　　　H. Walford Davies

Andante tranquillo

1. O
2. O
3. How

lit - tle town of Beth - le - hem, How still we see thee lie!
morn - ing stars, to - geth - er Pro - claim the ho - ly birth,
si - lent-ly, how si - lent-ly The won-drous gift is giv'n!

A - bove thy deep and dream-less sleep The si - lent stars go by.
And prais - es sing to God the King, And peace to men on earth;
So God im-parts to hu - man hearts The bless-ings of His heav'n.

*By permission of C. Morley Horder

Cast out our sin, and en - ter in, Be born in us to - day.

cresc.

We hear the Christ-mas an - gels The great glad tid - ings tell.

O come to us, a - bide with us, Our Lord___ Im - man - u - el.

70. ON THAT CHRISTMAS DAY MORN

Nancy Archer

Johannes Brahms, arr. W.L.R.

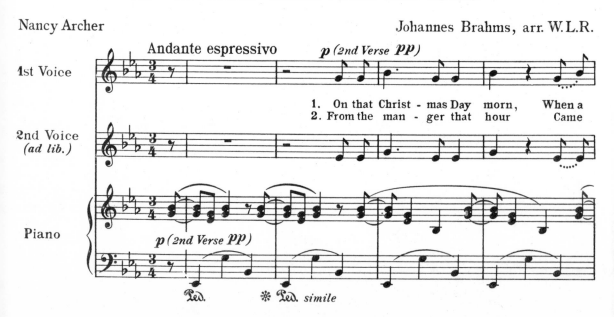

Andante espressivo *p (2nd Verse pp)*

1st Voice

2nd Voice
(ad lib.)

1. On that Christ - mas Day morn, When a
2. From the man - ger that hour Came

Piano

p (2nd Verse pp)

Ped. ✳ Ped. simile

new world was born, — All the hope of man-kind In a
God's love and pow'r, — And it comes now, to - day, To a

cresc.

man-ger lay en - shrined; And at this Christ-mas-tide Shall that new world a -
world that's lost its way; And as Christ's pow'r of old List'ning pro-phets fore -

cresc.

bide A-mong mil - lions on earth, As His spi-rit comes to birth.
told, So to - day list'ning men Can be pro - phets a - gain.

71. RING OUT, WILD BELLS

Tennyson

Edgar L. Bainton

Allegro maestoso

1. Ring out, wild bells, to the wild sky, The fly - ing cloud, the frost - y light: The year is dy - ing in the night; Ring out, wild bells, and let him

By permission of The Oxford University Press

true. 3. Ring in the valiant man and free, The larg - er heart, the kind - lier hand; Ring out the dark-ness of the land, ____ Ring in the Christ that is ___ to be. ____

72. THE THREE KINGS

Peter Cornelius
trans. H. N. Bate*

Peter Cornelius

Rather slowly *(the accompanying Chorale with breadth)*

1. Three kings from Per - sian lands a - far To Jor-dan fol - low the
p (How bright - ly shines the

point - ing star, And this the quest of the trav - el - lers three, Where the
morn - ing star! With grace and

new - born King of the Jews may be. Full roy - al gifts they bear for the
truth from heav'n a - far *p* Our

King; Gold, in - cense, myrrh are their of - fer - ing. 2. The star shines
Jes - se tree now blow - - eth.

* From the Oxford Book of Carols, by permission of The Oxford University Press

3. Thou Child of man — lo, to Beth-le-hem   The kings are trav - 'lling —

Thy   word,   Je —   su,

un poco più mosso

tra - vel with them!   The star of mer - cy, the star of

p un poco più mosso

In — ly   feeds   us,

rit.

grace, Shall lead thy heart to its rest - ing - place. Gold, in - cense, myrrh thou canst not

Right — ly   leads   us,   Life   be - stow _rit._ - - -

a tempo

bring; Of - fer thy heart   to the in - fant King,   Of - fer thy heart!

a tempo

- ing.   _f_ Praise, O   praise such love o'er flow - - - ing!)

The old Christmas tune 'Wie schön leuchtet' forms the accompaniment

73. THE VIRGIN'S CRADLE HYMN

Samuel Taylor Coleridge (1772–1834)

F. T. Durrant

74. THOU MUST LEAVE THY LOWLY DWELLING

(THE SHEPHERDS' FAREWELL TO THE HOLY FAMILY)
(Chorus from "L'enfance du Christ," Op.25)

English words by Paul England *

Hector Berlioz

In bar five and elsewhere, alternatives (always indicated by small notes) are given in the vocal Bass part
* *By permission of Novello & Co. Ltd.*

128

B.P.103

Guard ye well your Heav'n-ly Trea-sure, The Prince of Peace, the Ho - ly Child!

Guard ye well your Heav'n-ly Trea-sure, The Prince of Peace, the Ho - ly Child!

Guard ye well your Heav'n-ly Trea-sure, The Prince of Peace, the Ho - ly Child!

Guard ye well your Heav'n-ly Trea-sure, The Prince of Peace, the Ho-ly Child!

God go with you, God pro - tect you, Guide you safe - ly through the wild!

God go with you, God pro-tect you, Guide you safe - ly through the wild!

God go with you, God pro-tect you, Guide you safe - ly through the wild!

God go with you, God pro-tect you, Guide you safe - ly through the wild!

God go with you, God pro-tect you, Guide you safe-ly through the

God go with you, God pro-tect you, Guide you safe-ly through the

God go with you, God pro-tect you, Guide you safe-ly through the

God go with you, God pro-tect you, Guide you safe-ly through the

wild, guide you safe-ly through the wild! ____

wild, guide you safe-ly through the wild! ____

wild, guide you safe-ly through the wild! ____

wild,____ guide you safe-ly through the wild! ____

75. WHEN CHRIST WAS BORN OF MARY FREE

Traditional

W. L. Reed

* *Pedal notes (in smaller type) to be used for Organ accompaniment*
Copyright 1935 by W. L. Reed

Tenor Solo

2. Shep-herds be-held those an-gels bright, To them ap-pear-ing with great light, And said, 'God's son is born this night'.

molto cresc.

Glo - ri - a in ex - cel - sis De - o.

Glo - ri - a in ex - cel - sis De - o.

136

76. WORKERS' CAROL

Morris Martin   Paul Petrocokino

Slowly   *(First half of v. 2 in unison and faster)*

1. Cold - ly the night winds wing - ing, Soft - ly the shep - herds sing - ing,
2. Fierce - ly the blast fires burn - ing, Cease - less the wheels a - turn - ing,
3. Fount of the na - tions' heal - ing, Se - cret of peace re - veal - ing,

Hark, O you men of bat - tle,__ Ma - ry's__ Child is born._____
Have you no room, who la - bour__ On the as - sem - bly - line?_____
Through the world's dark - ness lead us__ Till Thy new day we see!_____

No room but in a man - ger, Come, Thou love - ly Stran - ger,
Ma - ry's__ Son be - side you Brings His grace to guide__ you.
Crown and__ Cross and Cra - dle, Scep - tre and Scourge and Sta - ble,

Born a - mong the cat - tle,__ Lord of the Christ - mas morn.____
Yea, come, Thou heav'n - ly Neigh - bour, En - ter this heart of mine.____
Tears and__ Tri - umph speed us__ On to Thy vic - tor - y!

B. P. 103

77. CHORALE PRELUDE on 'ES IST EIN' ROS' ENTSPRUNGEN'
(From 'Eleven Chorale Preludes for the Organ', Op.122)

Johannes Brahms

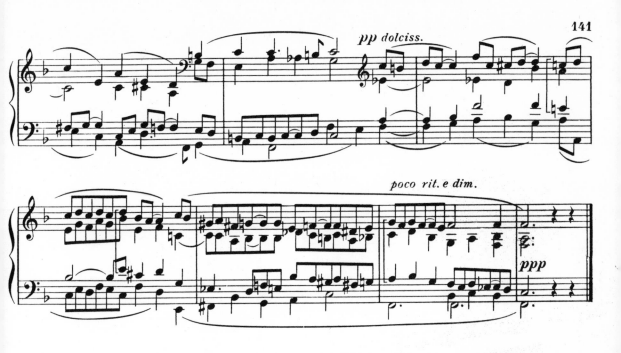

78. PASTORALE from the CHRISTMAS CONCERTO

Corelli, arr. W.L.R.

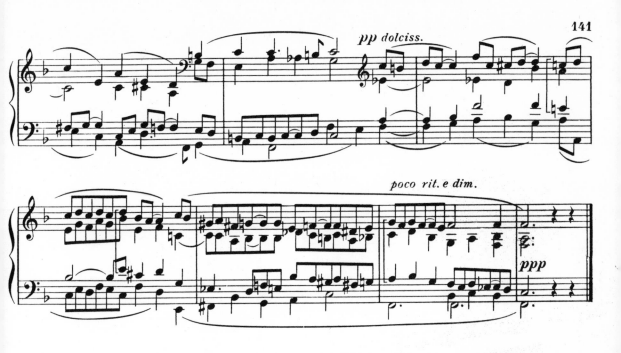

78. PASTORALE from the CHRISTMAS CONCERTO

Corelli, arr. W.L.R.

79. PASTORAL SYMPHONY from 'MESSIAH'

Handel

80. SYMPHONY from the CHRISTMAS ORATORIO

J. S. Bach

148